Michelle Kwan

Additional Titles in the Sports Reports Series

Troy Aikman
Star Quarterback
(0-89490-927-4)

Roberto Alomar
Star Second Baseman
(0-7660-1079-1)

Charles Barkley
Star Forward
(0-89490-655-0)

Terrell Davis
Star Running Back
(0-7660-1331-6)

Tim Duncan
Star Forward
(0-7660-1334-0)

Dale Earnhardt
Star Race Car Driver
(0-7660-1335-9)

Brett Favre
Star Quarterback
(0-7660-1332-4)

Jeff Gordon
Star Race Car Driver
(0-7660-1083-X)

Wayne Gretzky
Star Center
(0-89490-930-4)

Ken Griffey, Jr.
Star Outfielder
(0-89490-802-2)

Scott Hamilton
Star Figure Skater
(0-7660-1236-0)

Anfernee Hardaway
Star Guard
(0-7660-1234-4)

Tim Hardaway
Star Guard
(0-7660-1500-9)

Grant Hill
Star Forward
(0-7660-1078-3)

Allen Iverson
Star Guard
(0-7660-1501-7)

Michael Jordan
Star Guard
(0-89490-482-5)

Shawn Kemp
Star Forward
(0-89490-929-0)

Jason Kidd
Star Guard
(0-7660-1333-2)

Tara Lipinski
Star Figure Skater
(0-7660-1505-X)

Dan Marino
Star Quarterback
(0-89490-933-9)

Mark Messier
Star Center
(0-89490-801-4)

Reggie Miller
Star Guard
(0-7660-1082-1)

Randy Moss
Star Wide Receiver
(0-7660-1504-1)

Chris Mullin
Star Forward
(0-89490-486-8)

Hakeem Olajuwon
Star Center
(0-89490-803-0)

Shaquille O'Neal
Star Center
(0-89490-656-9)

Gary Payton
Star Guard
(0-7660-1330-8)

Scottie Pippen
Star Forward
(0-7660-1080-5)

Jerry Rice
Star Wide Receiver
(0-89490-928-2)

Cal Ripken, Jr.
Star Shortstop
(0-89490-485-X)

David Robinson
Star Center
(0-89490-483-3)

Barry Sanders
Star Running Back
(0-89490-484-1)

Deion Sanders
Star Athlete
(0-89490-652-6)

Junior Seau
Star Linebacker
(0-89490-800-6)

Emmitt Smith
Star Running Back
(0-89490-653-4)

Frank Thomas
Star First Baseman
(0-89490-659-3)

Chris Webber
Star Forward
(0-89490-799-9)

Tiger Woods
Star Golfer
(0-7660-1081-3)

Steve Young
Star Quarterback
(0-89490-654-2)

SPORTS REPORTS

Michelle Kwan

Star Figure Skater

DISCARDED

Barry Wilner

Enslow Publishers, Inc.
40 Industrial Road   PO Box 38
Box 398   Aldershot
Berkeley Heights, NJ 07922   Hants GU12 6BP
USA   UK
http://www.enslow.com

Acknowledgments

The writing of this book would not have been possible without the help and understanding of my wife, Helene; daughters, Nicole, Jamie, and Tricia; and son, Evan.

I would also like to acknowledge the contributions of: Nancy Armour, Richard Callaghan, Frank Carroll, Bob Dunlop, Shep Goldberg, Beth Harris, Karen Kwan, Heather Linhart, Marie Millikan, Bob Millward, John Nadel, Lynn Plage, Amy Rosewater, Gerri Walbert, Joseph White, and Sal Zanca.

Copyright © 2001 by Barry Wilner

All rights reserved.

No part of this book may be reproduced by any means without the written permission of the publisher.

Library of Congress Cataloging-in-Publication Data

Wilner, Barry.
   Michelle Kwan : star figure skater / Barry Wilner.
     p. cm. — (Sports reports)
   Includes bibliographical references and index.
   ISBN 0-7660-1504-1
   1. Kwan, Michelle, 1980– .—Juvenile literature. 2. Skaters—United States—Biography—Juvenile literature. 3. Women skaters—United States—Biography—Juvenile literature. [1. Kwan, Michelle, 1980– . 2. Ice skaters. 3. Chinese Americans—Biography. 4. Women—Biography.]
   I. Title. II. Series.
   GV850.K93 W55   2001
   796.91'2'092—dc21

                                                   00-009524

Printed in the United States of America

10 9 8 7 6 5 4 3 2

To Our Readers:

We have done our best to make sure all Internet addresses in this book were active and appropriate when we went to press. However, the author and the publisher have no control over and assume no liability for the material available on those Internet sites or on other Web sites they may link to. Any comments or suggestions can be sent by e-mail to comments@enslow.com or to the address on the back cover.

Photo Credits: AP Photo/Amy Sancetta, p. 71; AP Photo/Beth A. Keiser, pp. 13, 52, 81; AP Photo/Cliff Schiappa, p. 48; AP Photo/Eric Draper, pp. 58, 73; AP Photo/John Makely, p. 87; AP Photo/Kevork Djansezian, p. 30; AP Photo/Lynne Sladky, p. 76; AP Photo/Mark Humphrey, p. 62; AP Photo/Michelle Bridwell, p. 22; AP Photo/Paul Sakuma, p. 66; AP Photo/Susan Vranic, p. 44.

Cover Photo: AP Photo/John Makely

Contents

1 Perfection on Ice 7

2 The First Steps 15

3 Tonya, Nancy, and Michelle 27

4 Striving for the Top 40

5 Soaring to the Top 50

6 Olympic Silver, World Gold 64

7 The Big Balancing Act 78

Chapter Notes 91

Career Statistics 96

Where to Write and
Internet Addresses 98

Glossary 99

Index 103

Chapter 1

Perfection on Ice

Michelle Kwan's foot hurt. That was the last thing she needed at such an important time in her career. With the 1998 Olympic Games at Nagano, Japan, just three months away, Kwan was considered the favorite for the women's figure skating gold medal. Even though she had lost the United States Championship and the World Championship to Tara Lipinski earlier in 1997, Kwan had beaten Lipinski in their first meeting of the new season at Skate America in October.

A little over a week after winning Skate America with great performances, Kwan limped to victory in Skate Canada, another important international competition. She was lucky that Lipinski had not entered that contest. A doctor quickly diagnosed the pain and put her left foot in a cast. There was no way she could skate for at least three weeks. She withdrew from two major international events, the NHK Trophy in Japan and the Champions Series Final in Germany, so she could rest. Then she began training for the U.S. nationals that also serve as the Olympic trials.

Suddenly, her Olympic dreams seemed ready to crumble.

"I would have rather been healthy and skating well and go to Germany and compete, because that's where the competition is going to be," said Kwan.[1] She added she did not want the United States Figure Skating Federation to give her permission to skip nationals and automatically place her on the Olympic team.

"I don't want to go straight to the Olympics. I want the full experience. I want to earn it," she said. "I'm not feeling the best, but I'm not feeling like the pits. I think confidence goes in how you skate. I'm skating about average, so it's slowly coming."[2]

But would slowly be enough? And even if she could handle the physical pain, what about the mental stress of seeking an Olympic team spot without enough practice?

Kwan returned to the ice in December, but was

forced to cut short some workouts. She even left out some jumps during her run-throughs (practice programs), and changed some others to make them less painful.

But as the United States Championships approached in early January, Kwan really was not sure what she was capable of doing. She would travel to Philadelphia with some doubt—and with lots of determination.

"My confidence level is in the middle, and I'm trying to get it motivated to move up," Kwan said. "Hopefully, I can raise up my percentage of jumps and feel on top of the world again."

"It still hurts, but I think I can stand the pain. I'll be there at nationals. Even if it hurts, I'll still try."[3]

The National Championships would be the first meeting between Kwan, who was seventeen years old, and Lipinski, who was fifteen, since Skate America. Both were so far ahead of the rest of the world that they seemed certain to come in first and second, not only at the United States competition, but also at the Olympics in February.

So this would be the best test yet of where the two American teenagers stood. Would Tara Lipinski be able to repeat her national title performance of 1997, the first time she beat Kwan? Or

FACT

When Michelle Kwan won her second U.S. Championship in 1998, she became the first woman since 1989 to win back her title after having lost it. Jill Trenary did it in 1989.

would Kwan, injured foot and all, be able to hold off her younger rival?

Kwan would be attempting to win the competition despite dropping two of the easier triple jumps, the toe loop and the Salchow, from her programs. It simply hurt her left foot too much to do the takeoffs on those moves.

Getting rid of those moves meant substituting the more difficult triple flip, but it involved a right-footed takeoff and was not painful.

"You get more credit, it's harder and it's more consistent, so why not put it in?" she said. "Going into the triple toe is easier [than a triple flip], but it's not an option right now."[4]

Nor was dropping out ever an option. Michelle Kwan was going to make the Olympic team with her skating, whether that meant finishing first, second, or third. Whether she was injured or she was healthy, she was going to make it to the Olympics in Nagano, Japan.

"The injury hit me in the head and I said I would really enjoy myself," Kwan said with a laugh. "This is the Olympic year and I've been waiting for it since I was five years old."[5]

The anxiety got to her just before the short program, the first of two routines she was required to present at nationals. Worth one-third of the total score, the short program includes eight required elements. If a performer misses only one required element, her shot at a gold medal can be damaged. If more than one required element is missed, well, goodbye, gold medal.

Kwan could not fall asleep the night before the short program. Would she be rusty? How much would her foot hurt? Would she forget to do an element of the program? Would she be good enough?

She was not just good enough, Michelle Kwan's performance was just about perfect.

Looking calm and content, Kwan took the ice to a huge ovation from the crowd in Philadelphia. Always a fan favorite, she was even more popular now because of her battle to overcome her injury.

Kwan started off well and never struggled. When she began her combination jump, a difficult triple lutz-double toe loop, the crowd was silent, almost holding its breath to see if her injured foot would hold up.

She landed the combo with no problems, and then nailed every other portion of her routine. By the time she finished, the crowd was standing, cheering, shouting her name.

After a deep bow, she blew kisses to the fans, then waited for her marks.

What she saw made her gasp: Michelle Kwan

got seven perfect 6.0s out of nine marks for presentation.

"When the 6.0s went up, I thought, 'Am I hearing this right?'" she said. "Being in first, I could not have asked for more. I think it was one of my best short programs ever."[6]

Even though Tara Lipinski fell, she still was second in the short program. Kwan knew she had to also win the free skate, worth two-thirds of the total score, to recapture her national crown.

But now Kwan had more faith in herself. Although the foot still hurt, the pain was bearable.

Just as important, she knew she could skate well with the injury. Heading into the free skate, Kwan felt just about unbeatable. And she was. In fact, her performance might have been the greatest in the history of women's figure skating.

Certainly some of the judges felt that way: Kwan received eight perfect marks for artistry, the most 6.0s in a free skate at nationals for any skater—ever. In all, she had fifteen 6.0s out of a possible eighteen for artistic impression in her two routines.

Skating to "Lyra Angelica,"[7] a song about angels, Kwan hit six triple jumps, two in combination. But it was the beauty of her performance that had the crowd on its feet for nearly the entire four minutes,

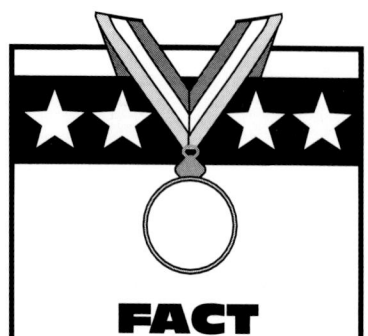

FACT

Kwan's fifteen perfect 6.0s at Philadelphia were more than all skaters combined in any other year. The previous high had been nine in 1988, awarded to Brian Boitano.

Michelle Kwan and her coach, Frank Carroll, react to the announcement of Kwan's perfect scores in the ladies free skate at the U.S. Figure Skating Championships in Philadelphia in 1998.

and had the fans chanting "6.0! 6.0!" as she awaited her marks.

"I just listened to the crowd and listened to the music and I thought of angels and clouds," Kwan said.[7]

Kwan said she was inspired by her childhood idol, 1988 Olympic champion Brian Boitano. She even blew a kiss to him as she left the ice.

Boitano, who was working for ABC television, is the only other skater to get eight perfect marks for a program at nationals.

"I knew before that the 6.0s were going to come up," Boitano said. "I just knew. I knew America would send her to the Olympics with a really strong win."[8]

Even her coach, Frank Carroll, was stunned by the marks. And nobody is a bigger Michelle Kwan fan than her coach.

"I thought it was one of her best moments," Carroll said of her performance. "It was not so much what she did, but the way she did it."[9]

What she had done was soar above the competition, above the arena, above the clouds, and given a heavenly performance.

Chapter 2

The First Steps

Even the great champions, even the Michelle Kwans, do not just put on their first pair of skates, glide onto the ice, and begin doing jumps and spins.

No, even the great ones have trouble getting the skate boots to fit or tying the laces when they start out. They find out very quickly that the ice is slippery and cold and wet. They discover that just getting around the rink is no snap.

It was no different for Kwan when she took her first steps toward what would be fame, glory, and a leading role in women's sports.

For one thing, she likes warmth, not cold. For another, she had rented skates that did not support her wobbly legs very well. And her feet hurt when she skated.

"But it also was great fun," she said. "Right from the beginning, Karen and I loved it."[1]

But sacrifices would have to be made for Michelle and sister Karen to advance as serious skaters.

Michelle's tight-knit family includes her mother, Estella, her father, Danny, her brother, Ron, who is four years older than Michelle, and Karen, who also would become a top-level skater and is two years older than Michelle.

There were no figure skaters in the Kwan family before Michelle and Karen took to the ice in 1985 after watching Ron play hockey. Both of their parents were born in China, where skating was not popular.

Danny Kwan's early years were ones of poverty, and he tells stories of waiting on line for food and of not attending school until he was eight years old because the family could not afford it. But his family moved to Hong Kong when he was eight, and Danny soon met Estella in school.

By the time he was thirteen, Danny Kwan was working to support his family. He had no intention of moving to the United States until, when he was twenty-two, he attended a family wedding in California. Unmarried and with few responsibilities

FACT

The song "Michelle" by the Beatles was one of the biggest hits for the most influential rock band in history. It also was one of Danny Kwan's favorites, so he named his second daughter Michelle.

back home, he stayed in the Los Angeles area, eventually opening a restaurant.

Estella was working in a hospital in Hong Kong when she tired of being around so much illness, so she changed careers and began working in television. When Danny returned to Hong Kong for a school reunion, they began dating. After they were married, they moved to California.

Danny claims he named Michelle after the famous Beatles song of the same name. He smiles widely when he says that.

One reminder of Michelle's bonds with her Chinese heritage hangs around her neck: a necklace of a dragon given to her by her grandmother. To Michelle, it means good luck.

While she is American through and through, Michelle Kwan has such strong family roots that she holds close the Chinese tradition of honoring her parents.

"I know the sacrifices my parents, and my brother and sister, too, have made for me and my skating," she said. "That is very important to me, to remember what they have done and be grateful."[2]

The Kwan girls needed only a few months of group lessons at the Rolling Hills Estates shopping mall rink before they were ready for private lessons. Skating was becoming expensive, but experts everywhere were telling the Kwans that Michelle and Karen had great futures in the sport. Danny and Estella needed to make some hard decisions.

First, the family had to accept the odd hours at which the girls would take private lessons from their first coach, Derek James. In order to work around their school schedules, Karen and Michelle would awaken at 4:30 A.M. and get to the rink in Torrance an hour later. The girls would even sleep in their skating clothes to save some time in the mornings.

Also, the Kwans had to figure out how often their daughters could compete at local events, and how quickly they should take the various on-ice tests to move up from one level of skating to the next.

Even more difficult was finding the money to pay for so many lessons, equipment, and costumes. Sometimes, the girls had to skip lessons because they could not afford them. One Christmas, Danny Kwan said the family could not afford a tree, so Michelle won one in a school contest.

For one nine-month period, Karen and Michelle went without a coach, practicing on their own. It was then that Danny Kwan decided to sell their house in Rancho Palos Verdes, move in with Michelle's grandparents in Torrance, and devote most of the profits from the sale to the girls' skating.

But Danny Kwan never wanted skating to be

about the money. He has made it clear to Michelle that there is much more to life than dollar signs.

"If you skate, you have to have proper respect for the sport and proper perspective," he said.

> You have to learn how to deal with winning, and learn how to stand up when you're losing. Every occupation has dignity to it. You have to be honest from your heart and dedicated all the time.
>
> Nowadays, people say, "Hey, you can win Olympic gold and so much money." That is very disruptive. She never talks about that, never thinks about that. We don't want to tell her to win this competition or this $50,000. That's kind of betraying what you go after. It has to come from within.[3]

Although they often wore hand-me-down clothes and used costumes and skated in second-hand skates, the girls were thrilled that they could continue. They became even closer, although they never were confused for each other: Karen always has been much taller than Michelle; Karen always was, as Michelle would put it, "more feminine," while Michelle was more of a tomboy.

And although Karen was the first to make the U.S. Championships, as a novice in 1991, it was the younger Michelle whose career would take off. That did not bother Karen at all.

"We've always been the biggest fans of each other," Karen said. "Nobody roots harder for me than Michelle and nobody roots harder for Michelle than I do."[4]

The girls had become so good that by 1992 they had outgrown the Torrance rink, and they began making a 100-mile trip into the California mountains to Lake Arrowhead. Ice Castle, a world-class facility, had public skating sessions on weekends, and the Kwans went there regularly.

Even though she had no official coach, Michelle was skating so well that she won one of the nine regional competitions on the junior level. When she won a bronze medal at the Pacific Coast, one of the three sectionals, she qualified for nationals, an amazing step for a coachless skater.

That presented yet another huge problem for the Kwans, because Michelle needed a coach to go to nationals in Orlando. Where would they find the money for airfare for a coach to travel across the country to Florida, for the coach's hotel room for a week, and for lessons? Fortunately, some influential people had noticed Kwan's talent.

People such as George Steinbrenner, owner of the New York Yankees baseball team, who had been a vice president of the U.S. Olympic Committee, were offering financial support to the Kwans.

Others, such as family friends Steve and Ming Li Hazen, and Helen McLaughlin, also supported the girls.

As for a coach, well, while the sisters were skating in public sessions at Ice Castle, the mother of former U.S. champion and Olympic silver medalist Linda Fratianne saw them. When Michelle qualified for nationals, Virginia Fratianne arranged for the girls to have a lesson with Frank Carroll, the coach at Ice Castle who helped Linda become a champion.

"I guess you could call it an audition," said Carroll, one of the most successful coaches in the sport's history. "But when I saw Michelle skate, I knew instantly she had that special something that could lead to being a champion—if she was willing to work hard enough."[5]

Working hard never was a problem for the Kwan girls, who moved to Lake Arrowhead to become students at the private rink. They received scholarships, meaning that the family no longer would have to struggle to pay for skating.

Karen and Michelle would live in the mountain community, go to school there—until Michelle began taking private tutoring—train there, and become world-class figure skaters there.

"She was very raw, but very dedicated," Carroll

Michelle Kwan waves after winning the gold medal in figure skating at the Olympic Festival in San Antonio, Texas, in 1993.

said. "There was no doubt in my mind she had what it takes in work ethic, and that she would work very hard to learn everything we gave her."[6]

Work hard, yes. But was Michelle enjoying the experience? Or was skating becoming too high-pressure for her?

One night, she told her father that she dreamed of skating at nationals and it made her so nervous it woke her up. She could not go back to sleep. That was not what Danny Kwan wanted to hear.

He told Michelle that skating always must be fun. If she lost that feeling, then figure skating was not worth continuing.

It was a lesson Michelle never forgot. Even though she puts in more time on the ice than nearly any other top-level skater, she does not lose sight of what skating means to her.

"I just like to have the feel of the ice," she said.

> I'm not really good about skipping a couple of days, because it's a weird feeling when you get back on. It's like, where's the ice? You feel like the ice is one foot lower.
>
> I like skating all the time. I always knew that in the summer, when other skaters relax, that is when I have time to catch up a bit, to sneak behind and get ahead.[7]

Soon, she would be far, far ahead of her peers.

At her first national championships, Michelle Kwan finished ninth at the junior level as an eleven-year-old, competing against skaters much older than she was. It was the first time she fully understood what a kid she actually was. It also was the first time she skated poorly in a big event.

But it provided a great lesson: do not rush things.

Unfortunately, she did not learn that lesson right away. It was good that Michelle did not lose any of her confidence after such a weak performance. But being patient, well, that was not one of her strengths at the time.

So she decided to take the senior-level test, even though Carroll said she was not ready. Michelle believed that, at the age of twelve, she was prepared to move up.

Ever since she watched the 1988 Olympics on television and saw Brian Boitano win the gold medal, Michelle dreamed of being an Olympian. Carroll told her some stories about Fratianne's trip to the 1980 Olympics. If she did not become a senior before the 1993 season, she would have no chance to qualify for the 1994 Olympics; she conveniently forgot that no U.S. skater so young had ever gone to the Olympics.

Carroll wanted her to wait and, in juniors, perhaps win the U.S. title, then the world crown.

Michelle had other plans, and when Carroll went to a coaching conference in Canada, she took the senior test. And passed.

Then she had to tell her coach.

"Frank wasn't happy," Kwan said.

> In fact, he flipped out. I thought he was going to stop coaching me. He stopped talking to me, and even though I must have apologized to him a hundred times, he stayed angry.
>
> But he finally calmed down and said that we couldn't change things and I would have to become even more dedicated to training. I'd have to learn how to be more of an artist and more of a performer.
>
> I told him I would do whatever he thought was needed to do. And we did.[8]

Kwan needed to make her jumps so consistent that they became second nature. She needed to master the spins and footwork her rivals already did so well. She had to look more mature on the ice, so that she was not considered a mere child by the judges.

"You really have to put all your mind and heart into it," she said. "Some people use their mind and not their heart. I think that's what separates a very good skater from the best skaters."

"When you see Brian Boitano, he gives everything. When he's on the ice, he just lets it go."[9]

Kwan let it all go the next season. She won

regionals and sectionals in her first try as a senior and finished sixth at the 1993 nationals, an incredible leap in the standings, even though she admitted she did not skate nearly her best.

The next season was an Olympic year because the International Olympic Committee changed the schedule. Beginning in 1994, the Winter Games would be held two years after each Summer Games.

Guess who was thinking about qualifying for the Olympics?

Kwan said,

> This is all my dream, and it's really come true. I always look at life as trying to enjoy every minute of it. If you're having fun doing something, keep on doing it. Life is really short. You never know what could go wrong.
>
> If you have fame for a minute, enjoy fame for a minute. If it comes again, enjoy it again. Because fame isn't always there for you. Maybe you'll peek out of the curtain and say hello and then goodbye.[10]

Chapter 3

Tonya, Nancy, and Michelle

At the age of thirteen, Michelle Kwan became involved in a real-life soap opera that would change the way people looked at figure skating.

Kwan already was a rising star in the sport. She was America's big hope for the 1998 Olympics, by which time she would be all of seventeen—considered the beginning of a woman's figure skating prime these days.

"We weren't even thinking about the 1994 Olympics,"' coach Frank Carroll said. "Our thoughts were of 1998, certainly."[1]

But much would change in the early weeks of 1994, and Kwan would, indeed, wind up in Lillehammer, Norway.

The season began in Dallas at Skate America, always the first major international event of the year. Kwan was invited after her sixth-place showing at the 1993 nationals in Phoenix, and after winning two lesser competitions, the Gardena Spring Trophy in Italy and the U.S. Olympic Festival in San Antonio, Texas.

Kwan did not expect to win Skate America, but it was an opportunity to compete against some of the best senior women in the world. It was also a chance to show just how much she had learned from her first year as a senior skater.

"It doesn't bother me to be younger," Kwan said. "When you're out there on the ice, you don't think about that. You're out there to skate."

"I know that being in senior ladies, I have to get better. I try to work hard, but I know I still have a lot of work to do."[2]

The most work needed to be done to her artistry. That might seem strange now, when Kwan is, by far, the most artistic skater on the planet, likely to earn 6.0s at any competition. Back then, however, she was a whirling jumping jack—she had mastered nearly every triple jump—with only a touch of style.

Coach Frank Carroll, who had worked with Olympians Linda Fratianne and Christopher

Bowman, knew just what his newest star student needed. Carroll said,

> It's nice to have your own personality when you skate and to share that with the audience. That's what Michelle has. She's not just an athlete on the ice. She has feeling and shows finesse in how she does things.
>
> She had to become more consistent and outgoing with it, and it's something that will come very soon. Then you will see a very special performer.[3]

Kwan already was showing bits and pieces of the smoothness and elegance that eventually would be the highlights of her performances. She played well to the fans, but it seemed a bit forced, which is only natural for such a youngster.

"The real hard work for her will be on maturity and beauty," said Carroll.

> We like the way the jumps are right now. She does not struggle to do any of them. The emphasis on jumping is great for Michelle, perfect for her. It is easy for her to do seven triples in a program. The skaters who are eighteen or nineteen years old who might spin better . . . it can be very difficult to do all those jumps.
>
> It seems gymnastics and figure skating are geared to littler bodies who do really hard stuff. The difficulty definitely has overtaken artistry.[4]

Coach Frank Carroll works with Michelle Kwan on the ice. As Kwan grew up and matured, she and Coach Carroll worked on giving her performances a sense of grace and beauty.

One of the top artists in the sport, Nancy Kerrigan, and one of the best jumpers, Tonya Harding, stood in Kwan's way for an Olympic spot in Norway. Both had won national titles and gone to the 1992 Games, where Kerrigan won a bronze medal and Harding finished fourth.

Kwan would finish seventh at Skate America, and while that does not sound like a strong showing, she skated well. But international judges did not know her yet, and they tend to be stingy with their marks for newcomers—especially with stars such as Oksana Baiul, then the world champion, and Tonya Harding in the field.

From there, Kwan went to the World Junior Championships in Colorado Springs. She won, joining the likes of Kristi Yamaguchi, Rosalynn Sumners, and Yuka Sato as a junior worlds winner. Those three went on to win senior world crowns, and Kwan hoped to do the same.

That was her last appearance as a junior. The next stop was the United States Championships in Detroit, where figure skating would be changed forever.

Kwan went to nationals hoping to make the medals podium, figuring that third place was possible. She also went there knowing that her older

FACT

Michelle Kwan says she remembers very little about her early years, except being jealous when her brother, Ron, and sister, Karen, were in school and she had to stay home. She also remembers liking candy and playing with stuffed animals.

sister, Karen, had passed her senior level test and, someday, might also be at nationals.

Before she left for Detroit in early January 1994, Michelle was told by Karen about a dream her sister had. Karen told her she would finish second and that Kerrigan would not skate, even though she was the defending champion and the United States' best hope for a gold medal at Lillehammer.

Kwan thought it was a crazy dream, but she did not forget what Karen told her.

On Thursday, one day before the women were to begin competition at Joe Louis Arena, practice sessions were going on at Cobo Hall next door. While most of the fans attending nationals—as well as the media and U.S. skating officials—were watching competition, Kwan and Kerrigan were working out in the smaller arena.

Kwan left the ice after practice and walked down a runway, stopping only to put her skateguards on. She heard someone ask Kerrigan, who was a few yards behind her, for an autograph.

As Kerrigan walked behind a curtain, Kwan headed for the dressing room. Then, she heard a scream from behind the curtain.

It was Kerrigan, who had been struck on the right leg by a man using a metal bar. As the man fled, people rushed to Kerrigan's side. So did Kwan, who saw Kerrigan lying on the ground, holding her leg and crying.

"It was unreal," Kwan said. "It was the kind of thing that happened in movies, but not for real."[5]

But it was real. Kerrigan was hurt badly enough to withdraw from nationals. While police investigated the attack, Kerrigan sat by and watched Harding regain the United States title she had previously won in 1991.

Newspaper and television reporters were not that interested in Harding's win. They were more concerned about whether the United States Figure Skating Association (USFSA), which runs the sport in America, would place Kerrigan on the Olympic squad anyway. If so, Kerrigan would join Harding at the Lillehammer Games one month later, and would bump the second-place finisher at nationals—Michelle Kwan.

"I was in a very strange position," Kwan said. "Of course, I wanted to go to the Olympics, but I wanted to earn it and I felt Nancy deserved to go. She didn't do anything to not belong there."[6]

It did not take long for the USFSA to make its decision. Moments after the women's free skate, the federation announced Harding would go to Lillehammer as the U.S. champion. Kerrigan would be awarded the second spot because the knee injury prevented her from skating at nationals. Should Kerrigan not be healthy enough by the time the skaters were due in Norway, Kwan would go.

"We're fine with the decision of the committee," said Carroll, who also witnessed the attack on Kerrigan. "Nancy's a great skater. Why should she be discarded? That would be playing right into his [the culprit's] hands."[7]

"I think it's fine," Kwan said of the decision. "They deserve to go to the Olympics. What I got was incredible already."[8]

She would get a lot more than she bargained for.

A few days after nationals, investigators began looking at Harding's possible involvement in the attack. Soon, they arrested her ex-husband, Jeff Gillooly, her former bodyguard, and two other men for planning and carrying out the attack.

While Gillooly claimed Harding approved of the attack, Harding said she knew nothing of it until after it happened. With the Olympics getting closer, there now were two decisions for the USFSA—and the U.S. Olympic Committee (USOC) which has final say on who makes its Olympic teams—to make.

One decision: Was Kerrigan healthy enough to compete at the Games? Decision two: Should

Harding be dropped from the team because she might have been involved in the attack on Kerrigan?

Kwan watched all of this from California, working on her programs just in case the Nancy-Tonya story wound up eliminating one or both of them from going to Norway.

"Everyone was fascinated by the story, which was all over the TV and in the newspapers," Kwan wrote in her book, *Heart of a Champion*, "the Olympics were right around the corner."[9]

On February 3, Kerrigan skated in Dennis, Massachusetts, for a USFSA panel that then cleared her to skate in the Olympics.

"If there were any doubt or any questions about Nancy Kerrigan's skating condition, she answered them for us this afternoon," said Chuck Foster, USOC secretary and one of the four judges who watched Kerrigan skate that day. "We expect that she is going to do very well in Norway."[10]

At the same time, the USOC was scheduling meetings about Harding. If the committee was certain she was involved in the attack, it would drop her and add Kwan to the team.

But the committee was not certain. Neither were investigators.

So just a few days before the Olympics would begin—the women's skating was scheduled for the last weekend of the games—Kwan received a phone call from the skating federation. She was told to pack her bags and head to Norway as an alternate. If Harding were removed from the team, Kwan would skate in the Olympics, four years earlier than she had planned—or dreamed.

Kwan had been training just in case. But she did not really expect to go to Norway. No one around her thought that would happen.

"I talked with her dad last week and he made the comment that he was never more proud of her than he was when she said Nancy Kerrigan deserved to be on the Olympic team," said Dave Cathalinat, principal of Mary Putnam Henck Intermediate School in Lake Arrowhead, where Kwan was a student. "That was before all the stuff came out about Tonya Harding."

"I said, 'I couldn't agree with you more.' I watched that interview, too. It was very typical of her. That's the kind of human being she is."[11]

Kwan found herself surrounded by reporters in Lake Arrowhead as the Tonya-Nancy saga grew. She wondered why the media was interested in her, but she also knew she could not become distracted—even with reporters waiting outside the Ice Castle rink where she trained. Some sneaked into the rink to speak with her.

Television shows such as *Hard Copy* and tabloid newspapers such as *The Inquirer* and *The World* were calling her house and coming to the rink seeking interviews.

Frank Carroll and Danny Kwan decided to hire a manager to deal with the media. They chose Shep Goldberg, who had seen the same kind of media hoopla when he worked with 1984 Olympic gymnastics champion Mary Lou Retton.

Goldberg took charge of public relations. Kwan thought she would be able to concentrate on skating.

When she, Carroll, and her father arrived in Norway, dozens of reporters were at the airport to speak with her. Photographers clicked their cameras. Television commentators stuck microphones in her face.

And they were not asking about how well she was skating or what she thought about perhaps being an Olympian. All they wanted to know was about Tonya and Nancy.

"I think Michelle handled it very well," Carroll said. "She just was herself. She had fun, and didn't let all of that affect her training."[12]

For a week, while the USOC and USFSA were sorting out the Harding situation, Kwan trained in Oslo, the capital of Norway, almost two hours away from the Olympic site by train. Kwan worked hard, even though she was nothing more than an alternate, never sure if the full practice sessions would lead to a spot on the Olympic ice.

"She was delighted to be there," Carroll said. "It was up to the USOC to disqualify Tonya up until the draw. If that happened, Michelle would skate."

"But she didn't expect to be at the Olympics in 1994, or to even be second in nationals. So she was in seventh heaven with how she did at nationals and with the trip to the Olympics. It was a lark, and she loved it."[13]

When the USOC, fearing a lawsuit, backed off and allowed Harding to skate, Kwan was not crushed. She remained in Norway, although as a spectator. She was not allowed to enter the Athletes Village or practice at the competition venue, because she was not on the Olympic team. She admitted it was a bit lonely to not be included in U.S. team functions.

"It was hard not being sure what would happen, whether I would skate or not skate," she said.

> When you are that close to something, sure, you'd like to compete. But I understood what was going on, and it really wasn't anything I could control. So I tried to have fun and make the most of it.[14]

Coach Carroll believes the Lillehammer experience was critical not only in Kwan's development as

FACT

Only once in the history of the U.S. Figure Skating Championships has the winner been stripped of the gold medal. In 1994, at Detroit, Tonya Harding won, then lost the title because she was involved in the plot to injure Nancy Kerrigan. Instead of giving the crown to Kwan, who was second, the U.S. Olympic Committee left it vacant.

a skater and a person, but in the way America looked at her.

"It made Michelle instantly a star," Carroll said. "She was the little girl who didn't get to go to the Olympics."[15]

Kwan also was thankful to the USFSA for paying all of her expenses in Norway. And she was thrilled to sit in the arena and watch Kerrigan finish second to Baiul; Harding was eighth.

Besides, there would be another Olympics for her to skate in. Maybe two.

Chapter 4

Striving for the Top

Michelle Kwan's strange year did not end at the 1994 Olympics. As the Tonya-Nancy story played out, Tonya Harding was banned from Olympics-eligible skating for life as a result of her role in the attack on Nancy Kerrigan. That eliminated Harding from attending the World Championships in Chiba, Japan, the following month.

Kerrigan also withdrew after her stressful season, and she soon retired from competitive skating. That left the future of United States women's figure skating in the hands of a group of teenagers. The leader of the pack was Michelle Kwan.

And a happy leader the thirteen-year-old was.

"I've wanted to do this all my life," Kwan said. "When I'm old, I'll just look back at everything and be happy."[1]

Kwan would not only attend worlds as a relative unknown to international skating judges, but she would also be faced with the pressure of needing to perform well to make sure the United States did not lose a spot at the 1995 World Championships. If neither she nor Nicole Bobek finished in the top ten at Chiba, America would have only one women's spot in the next year's worlds.

The last time the United States had fielded only one women's competitor in the World Championships was in 1984, but that was due to a mix-up with the paperwork naming alternates. One must go back in the record books to 1939 for another occasion on which only one woman from the United States competed, but, again, that was by choice, not because of a poor showing the previous year. It would really have been quite a disgrace for Kwan, as the leading woman skater in the United States, to have finished lower than tenth at worlds.

Would it bother Michelle? Nah.

"She does not get rattled," coach Carroll said. Technically, she's very good on the ice. She's warm and has a fun personality."[2]

Kwan, the youngest skater ever to represent the

United States at worlds, had spent some time working with Irina Rodnina, considered the greatest pairs skater ever. Rodnina, who retired in 1980 to become a coach, helped Kwan to be a more powerful skater. And helped give her a more mature look on the ice.

When Kwan arrived in Chiba, the Tonya-Nancy media frenzy had died down a bit. With Baiul and Kerrigan out, and the Olympic bronze medal winner, Lu Chen of China, sidelined due to a foot injury, it should have been easier for Kwan to get into the top ten. Instead, Kwan struggled in the short program, finishing eleventh after missing on her triple lutz jump. She needed a clutch performance to move up and keep that second world team spot for her country.

This was the perfect time for Kwan to get uptight. Instead, she relaxed. Wearing a huge grin as the crowd gave her a warm ovation, she responded with a superb performance.

Hitting two triple lutzes and skating cleanly, Kwan left the ice to loud cheers from the fans—and from her teammates and the American coaches. They all knew she had done well enough to move up, and the judges' marks confirmed it.

Michelle Kwan wound up eighth in her first

FACT

Kwan did not own a pair of new skates until 1995. Before then, she preferred used skates because they were comfortable—and her parents could not always afford new ones.

World Championships. She had done what her country had asked, too.

It was just a beginning, according to Coach Carroll.

"As a thirteen-year-old her body's going to change. She's going to have to watch her diet," the coach said. "She can improve her line, her stretch. Next year, we'll change her program to something more classical, artistic and intricate. It will test her artistic capacity."[3]

Rather than backing off, Kwan increased her busy schedule. She joined Champions on Ice, the tour that features the current world and national champions and other top skating stars. Kwan got to hang out with such greats as Brian Boitano, Oksana Baiul, Victor Petrenko and other skating legends.

That summer, she finished second at the Goodwill Games in St. Petersburg, Russia, behind world silver medalist Surya Bonaly.

In that event, Kwan had the best free skate of the eight veteran competitors and soared from sixth after the short program to the silver medal. It was the start of what she hoped would be a big year.

"I still have to improve my skating," said Kwan. "The jump that worries me the most is the triple loop. When I was out there I was thinking maybe I should double it, but if I don't do it here, then when

Michelle Kwan shows style, grace, and elegance on the ice.

am I going to do it? I had to get that thought out of my head."[4]

By the time she reached Skate America in Pittsburgh in the fall, Kwan was ready for a big year. It did not happen.

Maybe a fourteen-year-old is not ready to be a favorite, because Kwan was second (again to Bonaly) at Skate America, then wound up third at the Trophée Lalique in France and third again at the U.S. Pro-Am Challenge in Philadelphia.

But results were not the main thing on Michelle's mind in those events. She was building toward the United States Championships.

"Nationals is a very important step. I just want to go in there and pull off everything I can do, just do my best and not worry about anything else," Kwan said.[5]

Even nicer for Michelle and all the Kwans was the presence of Karen, who qualified for nationals, making them the first sisters in thirty-six years to skate together in singles in the top event in American skating. It also would be the first time since the 1992 Pacific Coast Junior Championships, with Michelle finishing third and Karen fifth, that they competed in the same event.

How would they handle that, especially with all

the attention it would get? Not that Michelle was unused to the spotlight by now.

"We probably won't talk that much," Michelle said. "We'll just focus on our own skating and not worry about any other skaters. In competition, we usually don't watch the skaters ahead of us and after we're done, we watch as much as we can."

"We hang around each other a lot, so if we have a problem we always talk it out."[6]

Added Karen, who also was coached by Carroll, "I envy her skating. I like to watch her, but it's not like jealousy. And if I'm having a bad day, she'll say, 'Don't worry about it. You can do it, I've seen you do it many times.'"[7]

So these senior national championships would be different from the other two for Michelle. She was not the only skating Kwan, and she was the favorite, which she admitted did not thrill her.

Kwan knew that Nicole Bobek and Tonia Kwiatkowski, both older skaters with more experience in seniors, were in good form. When Kwan bobbled on her combination jump in the short program, she slipped to third place behind Kwiatkowski and Bobek heading into the free skate. But if she could win the free skate, no matter what the others did, she would have her first national title.

FACT

A teddy-bear backpack was Michelle Kwan's constant companion in her early travels on the skating circuit.

Unfortunately, Michelle did not skate all that well in the long program, either. She went last in the final group, which meant she spent nearly forty-five minutes off the ice as the other skaters performed, followed by television commercials before the marks were announced. It was a very long wait. By the time she got onto the ice—more than an hour after Karen's free skate, which earned her seventh place—Michelle had tightened up.

Although she skated cleanly for most of the program, it did not have nearly as much energy as Bobek's routine. And when Kwan fell on the triple lutz again, she knew Bobek would win.

"I don't feel the pressure got to me. Going into it, I felt really confident and knew I could get through the program. I was really proud. I don't really care about overall standing."[8]

Still, she had been building toward becoming the American champion, and she had fallen short. All she could do was turn her attention to the World Championships.

Worlds were held in Birmingham, England. In the four weeks between nationals and worlds, Carroll added elements to Kwan's long program. He made it more difficult, putting in seven triple jumps.

But Kwan's shot at the gold medal ended even before the free skate, when she was fifth in the short

When Kwan fell while performing the triple Lutz in her long program, she knew there was no way she would win nationals.

program—even though she skated cleanly and better than at nationals in Providence.

"When I was walking here, I felt nervous and my hands were shaking a bit," Kwan said. "But my coach and my dad helped me when they said just go for everything. I went for everything and it turned out great."[9]

Things did not really turn out great. But they did go well enough to convince Kwan she would do something special in the free skate.

When she went on the ice for the free skate, perhaps relieved by the fact she was not a gold-medal contender, Kwan was more at ease than any time that season. She landed her first triple lutz cleanly, and took off from there. Every element—each jump and spin, the footwork and artistry—was strong.

As she finished, Kwan began crying and crying. She could not stop.

These were tears of pure joy for what had been the best program of her career. It did not matter to Michelle that Lu Chen won, Bonaly was second, and Bobek was third. In these worlds, she had proven to herself just how much she could do.

By next season, she just knew she would be unstoppable.

Chapter 5

Soaring to the Top

Even though her first season as a favorite did not turn out particularly favorably for Michelle Kwan, she headed into the 1995–96 campaign with the belief that major championships were there for her to grab.

Kwan's only victory in the previous season had come at a pro-am competition against second-level talent. She was determined that this year, beginning with Skate America in Detroit, would be very different. Her skating routines would also be very different. No more "cute" looks with ponytails and without makeup. No more of the little girl outfits and routines. Kwan wanted to show maturity. She wanted to be a bit mysterious. And she wanted to be more artistic.

A few weeks after the 1995 World Championships, she met with coach Frank Carroll and choreographer Lori Nichol. "I told Frank and Lori I wanted to portray someone who was growing up, and to show those emotions I was feeling," Kwan said. "I wanted a more mature and more artistic look. They felt the same way. And it kind of clicked right away."[1]

Kwan was growing, physically and emotionally. She wanted to be more beautiful as a skater, but she also wanted her programs to be meaningful—to her, to the judges, and to the audience.

The search for the right piece of music took several months. Carroll and Nichol found something they liked, but Kwan did not like it. She told them this music would need to have a special effect on her, to move her.

Coach Carroll has a vast knowledge of music, especially classical pieces. When he suggested "Salome" by German composer Richard Strauss, Kwan admitted she had never heard of it.

Her coach explained the story, which comes from the Bible. Salome does a dance called "The Seven Veils," and the king honors her. The dance is very

Michelle Kwan shows maturity on the ice. She wants her programs to be meaningful to her, the judges, and the audience.

mysterious and dramatic—exactly what Kwan was looking for.

"I listened to it for five minutes and I knew it was going to be a brilliant program," Carroll said. "Michelle loved it because the music's a little bizarre and she'd never heard it before. And when I told her the story of Salome, her eyes popped out of her head, and that was fabulous, because it was like a story she could skate and tell."[2]

Skate America would be where Kwan performed the new program first. She had worked extra hard each day on it until she not only understood Salome's dance, but she could convince the audience she was Salome.

"I wanted a story that you can show when you're performing," said Kwan, who wore a dark purple, midriff-baring costume for the routine. "It's like being an actress, trying to be Salome, and combining your artistry to the opera and performing it well. Not every day can someone go crazy in a program and do these weird movements."[3]

But would the audience go crazy or be puzzled by it? Would the judges accept it? Could this be the program that would carry Michelle Kwan to the top, or send her scurrying for something less strange?

An early answer came in Detroit. Although she

FACT

Lori Nichol, who is the choreographer for Michelle's programs, first impressed Kwan and Carroll when she brought a class of young skaters to Ice Castle. Nichol is from Toronto, as is Sandra Bezic, the choreographer for Kwan's main rival, Tara Lipinski.

trailed world champion Lu Chen of China going into the free skate, Kwan surged ahead—thanks to Salome.

The audience loved it, the judges liked it and, best of all, Kwan was satisfied with it.

"This is still the very early season," Kwan said of her first Skate America title. "I have to admit, I wasn't concerned about the placement. I just wanted to go out and know I could do it early and I did."[4]

Kwan knew she needed more competitions to improve the program, make it natural. At her next event, Skate Canada in Saint John, New Brunswick, she felt a little more comfortable as Salome. And even though she fell once in her free skate, she finished first for her biggest victory outside the United States as a senior.

"I'm very shocked and very surprised," she said. "It's like I'm not here right now—I'm floating somewhere. I haven't even gotten over winning Skate America yet. Now this. I can't believe it."[5]

Coach Carroll was beginning to believe this not only was the perfect program for Kwan, but that she would always be remembered for her portrayal of Salome.

"Salome was special," Carroll said. "No matter what Michelle does for the rest of her career, Salome will be special."[6]

Kwan's hot streak would continue at Nations Cup in Germany, her third straight major victory. She headed to the national championships in San Jose, California, once again as a favorite, even though Nicole Bobek was the defending United States champion.

Bobek always had a more mature look than Kwan did, mainly because she is nearly three years older than Michelle. But that had changed as Kwan settled into the role of Salome on ice.

"She was like a stick a couple of years ago," Carroll said of Kwan. "Now Michelle is a young lady in her body. She's strong and getting stronger."[7]

The way things were going for Kwan, it was unimaginable that another skater at the national championships would overshadow her. After all, this was going to be America's newest Ice Princess, the future Olympian and skating superstar.

Even more unimaginable was that Michelle would win her first United States crown and still not dominate the headlines.

But that was exactly what happened.

Kwan skated brilliantly at San Jose in a runaway victory. It did not matter that Bobek withdrew with an injured right ankle. Or that a new rival, thirteen-year-old Tara Lipinski, had introduced herself to the public with a great performance that earned her the bronze medal. Kwan was unbeatable.

Kwan's win normally would have been the first thing skating fans talked about at nationals. Except that in the men's competition, hometown skater Rudy Galindo capped a remarkable comeback by winning the gold.

Galindo, who had retired from the sport in 1995 because he did not have enough money to train, returned only because the United States championships were in San Jose. Then he put on the two best performances of his career.

Everywhere, fans, coaches, and other skaters could be seen crying tears of joy for Galindo. Kwan made sure she gave him an extra strong hug of congratulations, for she was moved by Rudy Galindo's victory, too.

Michelle also had hugs for sister Karen, who not only made the final warm-up at nationals, but wound up fifth overall. Even though Karen was not a great jumper, she had an artistic flair that reminded people of, well, her younger sister.

Michelle was so much better than the competition that she even allowed herself a slip of concentration near the end of her long program. Or maybe she was just so deep into portraying Salome that she was not ready to do a double axel to close the routine. Instead, she did a single.

But that was the only error, and Kwan swept away the judges. She was the champion of American women's figure skaters!

"Wow!" she said. "I'm so happy that I could skate my best and it would be good enough for this, to be the national champion. You want to do well for yourself and your family and your coaches, but then to have everyone like what you did is really great."[8]

Kwan had won every important competition so far, but there were two more left, two more to prove she was the world's best figure skater.

"Our philosophy is to never make predictions," Carroll said when asked how Kwan might do at the Grand Prix Finals and the World Championships. "People who do are nuts. Nine times out of ten, they're wrong."

"She has a good chance to finish in the top three if she skates the way she has all season."[9] At this point in her career, with Salome on her side, Michelle Kwan was capable of finishing in the top three in her sleep.

The Grand Prix Finals in Paris provided Kwan with another way of winning—rallying.

In the short program, Kwan fell on a triple toe

One of Kwan's biggest victories outside of the United States early in her career came at Skate Canada during the 1995–96 season.

loop and was just fourth heading into the free skate. Perhaps she was worried about a threat made against her—police had identified the man and kept him far from Michelle, who was surrounded by extra security for the event. Or maybe she was tired from a long season. Or she could have been looking ahead to worlds a month away.

"She was furious at herself," Carroll said. "It was just being sloppy. I mean, she never falls on a triple toe."[10]

Kwan now had to prove she could come from behind. Did she ever prove it, surging to the championship as the only skater who hit a triple-triple jump combination! She easily outskated Chen and European champ Irina Slutskaya of Russia, who would be her main rivals at worlds.

And then it was on to Edmonton, Canada, for the year's biggest event. Just a year ago, in Birmingham, England, she had proven so much to herself. Now, Michelle Kwan was ready to take on the worlds—and win.

But she also knew that Chen was the defending champ and that 1989 world winner Midori Ito of Japan—one of Kwan's idols—had returned. Kwan believed they were the favorites.

Ito, however, stumbled in the short program. Kwan did not, skating prettily to "Romanza" and showing the kind of footwork no other woman could match.

"I think my short program here was definitely the strongest I have ever done it," Kwan said after edging Chen. "Once I stepped onto the ice, I really focused on all the elements."[11]

Kwan would have to be even more focused for the free skate. Chen, who skated earlier in the final group than Kwan, was magnificent. She did not miss an element and became the first woman to get perfect marks at worlds, receiving 6.0s for artistry from the French and Hungarian judges.

"After I heard Lu's marks, I thought, 'Oh my God, I have to do a quad loop to win,'" Kwan said. "But then I settled down. I brought myself back to earth again and said, 'Heck, I'll go for everything.'"[12]

So Kwan hit seven triple jumps, including a triple toe loop at the very end of the program that was supposed to be an easier double axel. She flowed through the program, her footwork dazzling, her spirals taking her on one skate from one end of the rink to the other.

She felt as if she was Salome. When she was done and the crowd was on its feet, Michelle Kwan was on top of the world. But the judges would decide her scores.

When the marks came in, Kwan received two perfect scores of 6.0, from Japan and Bulgaria. Her technical marks—helped by the additional triple jump—were higher than Chen's were. That made a difference.

At fifteen, Kwan was the third-youngest world champion, behind Sonja Henie, a three-time Olympic gold medalist, and 1994 Olympic champion Oksana Baiul. With Todd Eldredge winning the men's event, the United States had both world singles champions for the first time in ten years, when Kwan's idol, Brian Boitano, and Debi Thomas took the gold medals.

"It's been a dream of mine, something I thought about doing, since I started out," said Kwan. "I can't really get it in my brain that I did it."[13] Nor could Chen believe she had lost.

"I think I skated my best, did my best in my long program, and the marks were given and the judges decide who wins," she said. "There was no Chinese judge on the panel and that might have had an effect."[14]

Coach Carroll, who now had his second world champion—Linda Fratianne won it in 1977 and '79—did not think the makeup of the judging panel mattered. It was Kwan's look, her command, her

FACT

When Kwan won the World Championships in 1996 in Edmonton, she was fifteen years old, the youngest American winner of the title. Tara Lipinski became the youngest champion the following year.

At fifteen, Michelle Kwan was the third-youngest world champion.

jumping skills, her maturity, and her elegance that won the crown.

"I think you have to be very athletic and do the difficulty," Carroll said. "But with the girls, the judges look for that artistic quality, and if you don't have a good look or choreography—without that combination, it is impossible to be a world champion."[15]

Kwan, of course, had it all. And now she was on top of the world.

Chapter 6

Olympic Silver, World Gold

The 1997 season had been a bad dream in which Kwan learned some valuable lessons. In Nashville, she had skated disastrously, making several major mistakes and losing her U.S. title to Tara Lipinski.

Brian Boitano, by now a friend, had consoled her. Kwan said he gave her excellent advice. He told her she was thinking too much about the mechanics of what she was doing instead of just enjoying herself. When she lost her world title to Lipinski two months later, she was far less upset. She had remembered Boitano's words and had skated better, despite the loss.

When she won back her national title in Philadelphia in 1998 with two sensational performances, she was thrilled. But, she still was not completely healthy as the 1998 Olympics approached.

The small stress fracture in her foot was annoying enough that she was forced to limit her practice time between nationals in early January and the February Olympic games at Nagano, Japan.

That disappointed Kwan, who wanted to be in Nagano from the very beginning to experience everything the Olympics had to offer. After her unfulfilling taste of the Olympics in 1994 as an alternate who never got to skate, this should have been her chance to mix with athletes from other sports and other countries. This should have been a time of sharing with the best winter athletes on the planet.

"I wanted so badly to go to the opening ceremonies and see some skiing and hockey and just be a part of it all," she said.

> But I also knew I had to be in the best shape to skate that I could possibly be, so it was the best decision for me to stay in Lake Arrowhead and train and get treatment for my foot.
> I would never have forgiven myself if I went to the Olympics not as prepared as I possibly could be, and as healthy as I possibly could be.[1]

So Kwan remained in California until more than

Kwan made the decision to remain in California until more than a week into the 1998 Olympics to give a stress fracture in her foot time to heal.

a week into the Olympics. She watched the opening on television—and felt a void.

"I wish I could have been there for my teammates, but I watched it on TV, so I kind of was there," she said. "I had therapy on my foot and didn't know if I was ready or not. I thought maybe I should stay home a little longer."[2]

Coach Frank Carroll thought it was the correct decision. He said,

> [I]t's wonderful to be part of the Olympic experience and it's fabulous to participate. But Michelle will feel most fabulous if she skates well.
>
> It was Michelle's decision [to arrive at the Olympics late]. . . . She has very strong opinions and feelings about things."[3]

Kwan also decided, with urging from Carroll and from her family, not to stay in the athletes' village. Instead, the Kwans took rooms in a downtown Nagano hotel.

While Tara Lipinski, her top rival for the gold medal, was taking part in all kinds of Olympic events, Kwan practiced at White Ring, the Olympic figure skating rink, then returned to her hotel. She did some shopping. She sent e-mails to her sister Karen who was a college student in Boston, and to her friends back home. She relaxed. But she never got a true feeling for the Olympic experience.

"It's important that she be comfortable and rest and get the sleep she needs," Carroll said. "I stayed in many an Olympic village and it's noisy and distracting."[4]

"I like to stay with my mom and dad and feel really comfortable," Kwan added. "I think I'll have the whole Olympic experience. I'll spend my free time in the village."[5]

In the end, the decision not to stay in the Olympic Village might have proved costly. On the biggest night of the Games, Michelle Kwan would come up just a bit flat, while Tara Lipinski would perform with the kind of spirit and energy that typifies the Olympics.

First, Kwan and Lipinski would face off in the short program. And just as they did in Philadelphia, they would finish first and second, with Kwan ahead.

To piano music by Rachmaninoff, Kwan seemed to float along the ice. She nailed all of her jumps—a triple lutz-double toe loop combination, a triple toe loop (the jump her injury forced her to drop for nationals) and a double axel. Her spirals, taking her from sideboard to sideboard, were elegant.

There would be no perfect marks, but she did receive all 5.9s for artistry from the nine judges.

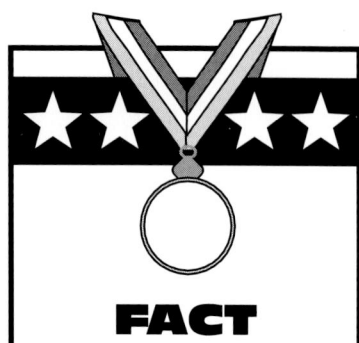

FACT

One banner hanging in the White Ring arena at Nagano said: "Michelle, Can I have a date?" Another banner was even more forward: "Michelle, Please Marry Me."

Kwan was first overall with eight judges, and she was more than satisfied with that—especially after having a short bout with nerves beforehand.

"I said to myself, 'I've done this so many times, I can do it now. I've done everything possible. I've trained hard.' I kind of knocked some sense into myself," she said.

"I heard people cheering and I thought, 'I'm in heaven.' People clapping, billions of people watching on TV and I'm skating. It's just me and the ice. When I'm on the ice, I don't think anybody can stop me."[6]

The women had one day of practice before their free skate, which would determine the gold medalist. Everyone believed it was between Kwan and Lipinski, with Kwan the favorite. After all, she had beaten Lipinski in their last five routines: short programs at Skate America, nationals and the Olympics, and free skates at Skate America and nationals.

But Kwan probably needed a perfect performance, one similar to the one she had had in Philadelphia, to hold off Lipinski, whom she expected to skate her best. Almost everyone else believed Michelle Kwan and Tara Lipinski would be superb.

"You expect them to skate perfectly," said Rosalynn Sumners, the 1984 Olympic silver medalist who was working for Turner Sports Television at Nagano, "and they do."⁷

Coach Carroll wondered about the unfairness of it all. Here were two great skaters, and one would be considered a disappointment for not winning a gold medal, even if she had the best night of her life on ice.

"When you consider Michelle and Tara, they both have been gold and silver medalists already. They both know the taste of winning," Carroll said. "You are going to win some, going to lose some, and if you can't cope with that, can't live with that, you are in the wrong sport."⁸

Kwan drew the first spot in the final group of six. After the skaters warmed up on the ice—both Kwan and Lipinski seemed slightly edgy, and their practice jumps were not very strong—everyone left the rink—everyone except one skater.

"Representing the United States of America," the arena announcer told the crowd, "Michelle Kwan."

Her routine began slowly, but unlike in other recent competitions, it did not build momentum. Kwan skated smoothly, elegantly, but without much liveliness. She seemed a little too careful.

Her marks were excellent for just about anyone, but merely very good for the favorite. She admitted skating as if she was protecting a lead. Kwan said, "In Philadelphia, I was more free. I was flying. Tonight, I

Michelle Kwan waits with her coach, Frank Carroll, to hear her free skate scores in Nagano, Japan, in 1998.

was more cautious, I took my time. I really enjoyed my performance, but it seemed like I was in my own world. I didn't open up and let go."[9]

Her coach noticed. "I just didn't think that spark was there," Frank Carroll said. "I don't want to criticize her tonight. I thought she did a great job. But I think there are things she can do better."

Still, Lipinski had not skated yet, and she would have to skate superbly to win. Which is just what Lipinski did, becoming the youngest women's Olympic champion ever at fifteen. Michelle Kwan took the silver medal.

Kwan was not sure how to react. She had come to Nagano expecting to win the gold. Silver was a great accomplishment. But it was not quite the color medal she had expected to win. She said,

> I was disappointed because I skated my best. And how come my best wasn't good enough? I'm really happy with what I've done and I should realize that. Like in twenty years, I can look back and be happy with myself and say, "Look kids, this is your mom. I tried my best. My best wasn't good enough that night, but I was able to win a silver medal."[10]

Oddly, in earning the silver, Kwan became a golden girl to many Americans. She conducted herself with grace, as did Lipinski, and gave credit

Michelle Kwan (left) kisses Tara Lipinski during the awards ceremony after the ladies free skate long program. Lipinski edged Kwan for the gold medal. Kwan finished with silver.

where it was due. And when Lipinski soon turned professional and Kwan said she would remain Olympic-eligible and probably try to make the U.S Olympic team for the 2002 Games, her following among the fans grew.

That was especially true six weeks later at the World Championships. Kwan came to Minneapolis with a fresh approach. She had no bad feelings about Nagano. The Olympics would be a highlight for her, now and forever.

"As kids you say, 'Third place is like kissing your mother, second place is like kissing your brother and first is glory.' It's not like that. It's very different," she said. "Every time I look at my medal, I feel like I've achieved something so high I can't say anything."

"I have no regrets about the Olympics. I feel proud of what I did. I tried my very best and I know that."[11]

Now, it was time for her best again, at worlds. Unlike many of the other top skaters—men and women—who skipped the '98 worlds, Kwan was in Minneapolis to defend her crown and remind the world just how special a performer she is.

"Personally, I think the title 'world champion' has a real ring to it and it is a great title, very, very meaningful and something to be very proud of the

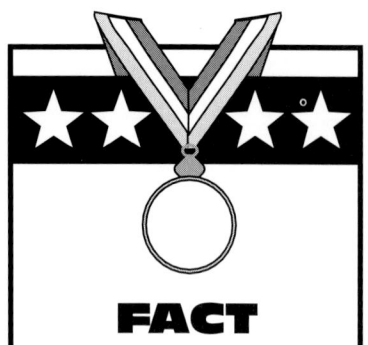

FACT

Michelle's silver medal was the seventh for an American woman at the Olympics. She joined Beatrix Loughran (1924), Tenley Albright (1952), Carol Heiss (1956), Linda Fratianne (1980), Rosalynn Sumners (1984), and Nancy Kerrigan (1994). Albright and Heiss won gold in their next Olympics as well.

rest of your life," Carroll said. "Yes, the skaters were required to do a lot of events this year, but the world championships are one of the most prestigious in the world and always will be. I don't see it connected to the Olympics."[12]

Kwan's foot still was sore, but her spirits were strong as she romped through the short program. When she landed the triple toe loop that had given her trouble ever since the injury, a huge smile crossed her face. As she spiraled the length of the rink with her leg extended gracefully behind her, the crowd at the Target Center went wild.

"When I stepped on the ice, I saw the American flags and banners and I wanted to give to the audience the joy and freedom I have on the ice," Kwan said. "I felt like they were carrying me through, and that was really nice."[13]

Even nicer was the thought that another world championship, and a fitting finish to her up-and-down year, was waiting. All Kwan had to do was what she does best—skate superbly.

No sweat.

Although she cut a triple Salchow to a double and fell on a double axel, Kwan was so much better than the other skaters that she still swept the judging panel. The win was her third in four competitions during the season, including her

The 1998 Olympics were not the first time that Kwan came in second to Tara Lipinski. After the World Figure Skating Championships in 1997, Lipinski and Kwan displayed their medals.

historic performance at Philadelphia. The only place she did not win was in Nagano.

As she looked back on the biggest, busiest season of her career, Kwan knew she could not rest on what she had accomplished. In sports, you cannot look back, and as she peered into the future, here was what Michelle Kwan saw:

> I think people are improving and I feel I have stayed the same in the technical part. I feel I'm going to have a couple months this year to really concentrate on improving and doing more difficulty in my programs. I want time for myself to really train hard and keep on improving.
>
> There are lots of skaters coming up and some of them will be doing triple axels and four triple-triples. And those little kids will be very artistic and have all the elements. I've got to keep up and ride the wave.[14]

Chapter 7

The Big Balancing Act

The first two years after an Olympics are the toughest ones for a figure skater. Michelle Kwan had her sights set on the 2002 Salt Lake City Games, but they were such a long way off.

And if there is one thing Michelle Kwan always has needed, it's been a challenge. So Kwan decided to challenge herself in many ways. She would become a role model, a fulltime student and, of course, be the best skater she could be. "Doing nothing but skating can make you crazy," she said. "I didn't want to be one-sided. Now, at least, I have distractions. Maybe too many."[1]

Kwan had become even more popular because of the gracious way she handled losing to Tara Lipinski at the Nagano Olympics. Within a year, such companies as Chevrolet, Walt Disney, Yoplait Yogurt, United Airlines, Campbell's Soup and Caress soap had signed up Kwan to use and promote their products. She began writing a series of instructional books for Disney's Buena Vista publishing division, and had a deal for television specials on ABC.

She credited the way she responded to coming in second at Nagano.

"People were amazed to see me still smiling—even though I didn't win. I became a role model to some that night," she said. "Here, I'd been chasing a dream since I was five years old and didn't achieve it. Yet I was still happy."[2]

To stay happy, she knew she had to focus on the most important thing in her life—skating.

"If I capitalized on everything that came my way, I would be a mess mentally," she said. "Skating is my first love. Everything else is extra."[3]

With that in mind, she set about having a big 1998–99 season. That meant winning nationals and worlds again.

First, Kwan, entered—and won—several lesser events, including the Goodwill Games in New York and the World Pro Championships, which for one year were opened to all skaters, with the blessing of the International Skating Union.

FACT

Michelle Kwan refuses to endorse any product she does not or would not use, and will not do commercials for any alcoholic products.

Heading to Salt Lake City for the national championships, Kwan was on a nine-event winning streak, the second time in her career she had gone that long undefeated. Except for a third place at the Centennial on Ice in Russia in early 1996 (where she was ill), Kwan had not finished below second in thirty-two competitions.

For inspiration at nationals, all Kwan had to do was look around. The United States Championships were being held in the Delta Center, where the 2002 Olympics would be staged. This was sort of a test run for those Games. What better than to win on the ice where, three years later, she hoped to cap her career with another great Olympic performance?

Kwan also could see the wave of the future as she gazed around the arena. At eighteen, she already was the "old lady" of American skating, with her top opponents—Naomi Nari Nam and Sarah Hughes—both fresh out of juniors.

Kwan said with a laugh,

> Yeah, they're getting younger and more athletic. But I'm not ready for a wheelchair or retirement. I don't pay a lot of attention to people who are coming up. You know there are people out there, working just as hard as you, maybe even harder. You have to be on top of your game, because you just never know.[4]

The years following the 1998 Olympics were challenging for Kwan as she set her sights on the 2002 Olympics.

Added her coach, Frank Carroll, "These young ladies will be excellent skaters in time. But they have much to do before they reach the level of maturity and performance and artistry of a Michelle Kwan."[5]

The difference between Kwan and the other skaters was clear at nationals, where Kwan might have won wearing army boots and double blades. It was never close, although Nam and Hughes, both thirteen, thrilled the crowd with their jumps and youthful energy.

But it was Kwan's show.

Skating her free program to "Ariane," Kwan simply floated above the competition. She hit six triple jumps, including the triple toe loop-triple toe loop combination that had given her trouble throughout her career. Even though she fell on a triple lutz, she won with ease.

It was her third United States title, but considering the weakness of the rest of the field, it did not prove much.

That would not be the case at the 1999 World Championships in Helsinki, Finland. Kwan would face the top skaters from Russia, France, Germany, and Japan. She had to be at her best. But she wasn't.

A head cold limited Kwan, and so did the new schedule that required every skater to go through a qualifying round, then a short program, then the free skate.

Russian Maria Butyrskaya, who regularly had lost to Kwan for four years, edged a sluggish Kwan for the gold. Carroll complained about the schedule.

"If you have forty or fifty skaters . . . then some of those skaters should not be here," he said. "The reason for the qualification is to more or less weed them out, but I don't think if you're probably one of the top three, four or five skaters in the world that you need to be weeded out."[6]

For the third straight year, Kwan had not reached all of her goals. Maybe she needed a break from the constant grind of focusing on skating, just skating.

Actually, that was exactly what she had been thinking about for more than a year. And she had the perfect plan. She would go to college. Her choice was UCLA, which was not far from home. But for a girl who had been taught by private tutors since she was thirteen, it really was in a whole different world.

Kwan was an excellent student. She had won the 1997 Dial Student Athlete of the Year award given to the top student-athlete in the United States. But there would be no home study this time. She would live in the dorms, playing the part of fulltime college student. Said Kwan,

> It was really hard. A lot of people told me don't do it. Skate and just worry about that. For me, education is important. I can't put skating on hold, nor do I want to be a twenty-six-year-old freshman.
>
> For me, the key part is when I'm skating I can't think about school, and when I'm in school, I can't think about skating.
>
> Since the eighth grade I've had a tutor and schooling always was on a one-on-one basis. I never had the high school experience, and I hope to make up for it and go for the full college experience.[7]

While Kwan carefully guarded her course schedule for security reasons, she had a great time in the 1999 fall semester at UCLA. She went to ball games. She hung out in the cafeteria and on campus. She became a typical coed who just happened to be a World Champion and Olympic medalist.

"I wanted the whole experience, the whole nine yards," she said. "I realize this [skating] is only a sport and there are greater things in life than doing a triple lutz. I appreciate that every day."[8]

What she could not appreciate was the struggle she was going through on the ice. Although she won Skate America early in the season, then was first at

FACT

One thing Michelle Kwan would like to see eliminated from the World Figure Skating Championships is the qualifying round. She believes she lost the 1999 world title because having to qualify before becoming ill weakened her.

Skate Canada, Kwan was not skating at nearly the level she had reached in past years. Privately, her coach felt that Kwan needed to spend more time on the ice.

Carroll had even more to worry about when Kwan finished second to Russia's Irina Slutskaya at the Grand Prix finals in Lyon, France. While Slutskaya and others were doing plenty of triple-triple combinations, Kwan was not. She had little time to practice them and no time to perfect them.

Surely, Kwan would rebound at nationals in Cleveland three weeks later.

Well, no. Instead, she fell in the short program on a triple toe loop. It was a shock. She had not fallen on this relatively simple jump in four years. The mistake nearly cost her the chance at a fourth United States crown. Kwan was third behind a new sensation from the United States, Sasha Cohen, and Sarah Hughes.

"I really feel I have to up the ante," said Kwan. "It's, I think, my seventh nationals and I feel ancient next to these people."[9]

Having been around for so long would actually help Kwan. When she skated decently, but not great, in her long program, and neither Cohen nor Hughes did anything spectacular, Kwan's reputation helped her with the judges. Despite falling on a triple loop and not performing anywhere near her best, Kwan won her fourth United States Championship—more than Dorothy Hamill, Kristi Yamaguchi, Jill Trenary or Rosalynn Sumners had ever won.

People were beginning to compare the Kwan of 2000 to previous Kwans instead of to her current competition. And that was not fair to Michelle Kwan.

"I don't think any of you really understand the pressure it takes to defend the national senior ladies title," Coach Carroll said.

> It's not a walk in the park and I think a lot of times people get the impression that Michelle is just going to walk in here and breeze through the title. It is very difficult to win, it is very, very difficult to hold and doing it is very, very nerve-racking.[10]

Once again, Kwan felt she was being challenged. She needed to re-establish herself as the world's best female skater. So she moved out of the UCLA dorm into private housing, took only one course in the spring semester and spent six weeks of extra hard training to get ready for the World Championships in Nice.

During those workouts, she concentrated on the triple toe loop-triple toe loop. She had to have it to beat Slutskaya and Butyrskaya.

Kwan may have won a silver medal at the 1998 Olympics. But, she would have to keep improving if she was going to get the better of the young competitors at the 2002 Games.

But the Russians outskated her in the qualifying round and the short program. That meant she needed to rally from third place by winning the free skate. With her competitive juices flowing, Kwan hit the ice with the kind of mindset that has made her a champion.

"Everyone kept saying, she has to do the triple-triple, she has to up the ante," Kwan said. "This is the first competition where I went out on the ice and pushed and pushed and pushed through the entire four minutes."[11]

She pushed so hard and so well—including landing the triple-triple—that she soared past Butyrskaya and Slutskaya. She soared right back to the top, as the first skater to recapture the world title twice.

"It feels very satisfying," Kwan said. "I was hearing people saying, 'Oh, she's over, oh, she's deteriorating.' To come back stronger for the World Championships, that's why it feels really good."[12]

But what about the 2002 Olympics, which are just around the corner now?

"Why not?" she said. "I'll have another shot. But it's not going to kill me if I never get a gold. How can you say that six minutes at the Olympics should decide whether you have a happy life?"[13]

Michelle Kwan had a very happy 2000–01 season, and as she thought about the rapidly approaching Salt Lake City Games, she saw all sorts of great possibilities. The last four women who went to the Olympics as world champions took home the Olympic gold medal. After adding her fourth world crown in Vancouver in March 2001, Kwan was sure she could keep that streak going. "Is that true?" she asked. "Wow! I'd really like to keep it that way."[14]

Although she lost to Russia's Irina Slutskaya at Skate Canada and in the Grand Prix finals, Kwan beat Slutskaya when it counted most, at worlds. By winning for the fourth time, she had equaled Katarina Witt's achievement and passed Peggy Fleming. Kwan also was the first woman since Kristi Yamaguchi in 1991–92 to win consecutive world championships.

Kwan's season began well with her fourth straight Skate America crown. But then she finished second to Slutskaya at Skate Canada and critics wondered if her programs were too easy.

Kwan did not do a triple jump combination in capturing her fifth U.S. championship—as many titles as the great Peggy Fleming, and more than Tara Lipinski, Kristi Yamaguchi and Nancy Kerrigan combined. Then, she came in second to Slutskaya at the Grand Prix finals, and wound up an underdog for worlds.

But her superb free skate, in which she conquered the triple-triple problem as well as Slutskaya, stamped Kwan as the woman to beat in Salt Lake City.

When the 2002 Olympics arrived, Kwan started off strong. At the end of the short programs, she stood in first place. Then in the long program, fellow American Sarah Hughes put on a show. Hughes landed her first double Axel and then her trademark triple Salchow-triple loop combination. Midway through her program, she landed her second triple-triple—this one a toe loop-loop combination.

Hughes earned mostly 5.8s and a couple of 5.7s. These were strong scores, but there was still room for Kwan to pass her. However, Kwan was unable to complete her triple toe-triple toe combination at the beginning of her program. She then fell on a triple flip. Hughes jumped from forth place all the way to first to earn the gold medal. Kwan finished third overall and took home the bronze.

Although she had not succeeded in her quest for the gold, she still managed to earn her second Olympic medal, which was quite an accomplishment. Clearly, Michelle Kwan has proven herself as one of the greatest women's figure skaters.

Chapter Notes

Chapter 1. Perfection on Ice

1. Nancy Armour, "Kwan Injury," The Associated Press electronic wire story, December 22, 1997.

2. Ibid.

3. Nancy Armour, "Going for Gold," The Associated Press electronic wire story, January 3, 1998, Philadelphia, Pa.

4. Author interview of Michelle Kwan, January 7, 1998, Philadelphia, Pa.

5. Ibid.

6. Author interview of Michelle Kwan, January 9, 1998, Philadelphia, Pa.

7. Ibid.

8. Ibid.

9. Ibid.

Chapter 2. The First Steps

1. Author interview of Michelle Kwan, October 29, 1999, Colorado Springs, Colo.

2. Ibid.

3. Steve Wilstein, "Michelle Kwan," The Associated Press electronic wire story, March 18, 1996.

4 Author interview of Karen Kwan, February 11, 1995, Providence, R.I.

5. Author interview of Frank Carroll, October 30, 1999, Colorado Springs, Colo.

6. Ibid.

7. Author interview of Michelle Kwan, March 23, 1996, Edmonton, Alberta, Canada.

8. Author interview of Michelle Kwan, October 29, 1999, Colorado Springs, Colo.

9. Author interview of Michelle Kwan, March 23, 1996, Edmonton, Alberta, Canada.

10. Steve Wilstein, "Michelle Kwan," The Associated Press, electronic wire story, March 18, 1996.

Chapter 3. Tonya, Nancy, and Michelle

1. Author interview of Frank Carroll, October 30, 1999, Colorado Springs, Colo.

2. Author interview of Michelle Kwan, October 21, 1993, Dallas, Tex.

3. Author interview of Frank Carroll, October 21, 1993, Dallas, Tex.

4. Ibid.

5. Author interview of Michelle Kwan, January 8, 1994, Detroit, Mich.

6. Ibid.

7. Author interview of Frank Carroll, January 8, 1994, Detroit, Mich.

8. Author interview of Michelle Kwan, January 8, 1994, Detroit, Mich.

9. Michelle Kwan, *Heart of a Champion* (New York: Scholastic, Inc., 1997), p. 68.

10. The Associated Press, "Kerrigan Attack," electronic wire story, February 3, 1994.

11. John Nadel, "Michelle Kwan," The Associated Press electronic wire story, February 5, 1994.

12. Author interview of Frank Carroll, October 30, 1999, Colorado Springs, Colo.

13. Ibid.

14. Author interview of Michelle Kwan, February 12, 1995, Providence, R.I.

15. Author interview of Frank Carroll, October 30, 1999, Colorado Springs, Colo.

Chapter 4. Striving for the Top

1. Louinn Lota, "Figure Skating-Kwan," The Associated Press electronic wire story, March 9, 1994.

2. Ibid.

3. Ibid.

4. Joseph White, "Goodwill Games," The Associated Press electronic wire story, August 6, 1994.

5. Beth Harris, "Figure Skating-Kwan," The Associated Press electronic wire story, February 3, 1995.

6. Ibid.

7. Ibid.

8. Author interview of Michelle Kwan, February 11, 1995, Providence, R.I.

9. Robert Millward, "World Skating—Kwan," The Associated Press electronic wire story, March 10, 1995.

Chapter 5. Soaring to the Top

1. Author interview of Michelle Kwan, January 19, 1996, San Jose, Calif.

2. Steve Wilstein, "Michelle Kwan," The Associated Press electronic wire story, March 18, 1996.

3. Ibid.

4. The Associated Press, "Skate America," electronic wire story, October 28, 1995.

5. The Associated Press, "Skate Canada," electronic wire story, November 3, 1995.

6. Author interview of Frank Carroll, October 30, 1999, Colorado Springs, Colo.

7. Wilstein, "Michelle Kwan," The Associated Press electronic wire story, March 18, 1996.

8. Ibid.

9. Ibid.

10. Author interview of Frank Carroll, February 24, 1996, Paris, France.

11. Author interview of Michelle Kwan, March 23, 1996, Edmonton, Alberta, Canada.

12. Author interview of Michelle Kwan, March 24, 1996, Edmonton, Alberta, Canada.

13. Ibid.

14. Ibid.

15. Author interview of Frank Carroll, March 24, 1996, Edmonton, Alberta, Canada.

Chapter 6. Olympic Silver, World Gold

1. Author interview of Michelle Kwan, April 3, 1998, Minneapolis, Minn.

2. Author interview of Michelle Kwan, February 10, 1998, Nagano, Japan.

3. Author interview of Frank Carroll, February 10, 1998, Nagano, Japan.

4. Ibid.

5. Author interview of Michelle Kwan, February 11, 1998, Nagano, Japan.

6. Author interview of Michelle Kwan, February 18, 1998, Nagano, Japan.

7. Author interview of Rosalynn Sumners, February 19, 1998, Nagano, Japan.

8. Author interview of Frank Caroll, February 19, 1998, Nagano, Japan.

9. Author interview of Michelle Kwan, February 20, 1998, Nagano, Japan.

10. Ibid.

11. Author interview of Michelle Kwan, April 3, 1998, Minneapolis, Minn.

12. Author interview of Frank Carroll, March 25, 1998, New York.

13. Author interview of Michelle Kwan, April 3, 1998, Minneapolis, Minn.

14. Author interview of Michelle Kwan, April 5, 1998, Minneapolis, Minn.

Chapter 7. The Big Balancing Act

1. David Oliver Relin, "Skating Through School," *React* magazine, February 7–13, 2000, p. 10.

2. Ibid.

3. Bruce Horvitz, "Cover Story," *USA Today*, February 9, 2000.

4. Author interview of Michelle Kwan, February 13, 1999, Salt Lake City, Utah.

5. Author interview of Frank Carroll, February 13, 1999, Salt Lake City, Utah.

6. Jim Heintz, "World Skating," The Associated Press electronic wire story, March 29, 1999, Helsinki, Finland.

7. Author interview of Michelle Kwan, April 14, 1999, New York.

8. Author interview of Michelle Kwan, February 3, 2000, Cleveland, Ohio.

9. Author interview of Michelle Kwan, February 12, 2000, Cleveland, Ohio.

10. Author interview of Frank Carroll, February 13, 2000, Cleveland, Ohio.

11. Author interview of Michelle Kwan, April 1, 2000, Nice, France.

12. Ibid.

13. Relin, p. 10.

14. Author interview of Michelle Kwan, March 24, 2001, Vancouver, British Columbia, Canada.

Career Statistics

	Competitive Highlights	
2002	Olympic Games	3rd
2001	World Championships	1st
2001	Grand Prix Finals	2nd
2001	United States Championships	1st
2000	Skate Canada	2nd
2000	Skate America	1st
2000	World Championships	1st
2000	United States Championships	1st
1999	Skate America	1st
1999	World Championships	2nd
1999	United States Championships	1st
1998	World Pro Championships	1st
1998	Goodwill Games	1st
1998	World Championships	1st
1998	Olympic Games	2nd
1998	United States Championships	1st
1997	Skate Canada	1st
1997	Skate America	1st
1997	World Championships	2nd
1997	Champions Series Final	2nd

Career Statistics (cont.)

	Competitive Highlights	
1997	United States Championships	2nd
1996	Trophée Lalique	1st
1996	Skate America	1st
1996	World Championships	1st
1996	Champions Series Final	1st
1996	United States Championships	1st
1995	Nations Cup	1st
1995	Skate Canada	1st
1995	Skate America	1st
1995	World Championships	4th
1995	United States Championships	2nd
1994	Trophée Lalique	3rd
1994	Skate America	2nd
1994	Goodwill Games	2nd
1994	World Championships	8th
1994	United States Championships	2nd
1994	World Junior Championships	1st
1993	Skate America	7th
1993	United States Junior Championships	6th

Where to Write Michelle Kwan

Ms. Michelle Kwan
c/o United States Figure Skating
Association (USFSA)
20 First Street
Colorado Springs, CO 80906

Internet Addresses

United States Figure Skating Association
<http://www.usfsa.org/>

International Skating Union (ISU)
<http://www.isu.org>

Glossary

compulsory figures—The tracing of figure eights on the ice. These figures are no longer done in competition.

double axel—A difficult jump in competition that requires an extra half turn in the air. It is a two-and-a-half revolution jump. The axel is the only jump that begins from the forward outside edge of the skate. It is landed on the back outside edge of the opposite foot.

figure eight—A skating pattern in which a performer's motions form the shape of the number eight on the ice.

free skate—The second portion of competition for solo and pairs skaters. It is worth two-thirds of the skater's total score, and skaters may perform anything they choose—within the rules of figure skating.

intermediate level—The easiest level of skating for a serious figure skater. The novice level follows this level.

International Skating Union (ISU)—The governing body for international figure skating and speed skating.

junior level—The level of skating for serious figure skaters that follows novice level.

long program—*See also*, free skate.

National Championships—The event in which the top novice, junior, and senior level skaters compete for United States titles.

novice level—The level of skating for serious figure skaters that follows intermediate level.

pairs—A team of skaters composed of one male and one female. The team performs together in competitions. Pairs skating differs from ice dancing in that in pairs, skaters are permitted to do lifts above the shoulder, throws, and jumps.

quadruple jump—Any jump requiring four turns in the air.

regionals—The first level of competition on the way to nationals.

sectionals—The level that follows regionals. Medal winners in sectionals automatically go to the national championships.

senior level—The highest level of skating for serious figure skaters.

stroke—The method that skaters use to progress across the ice. Even advanced skaters like Michelle Kwan take stroking classes to build power and speed.

technical program—The first of two programs skated by solo and pairs skaters. It is worth one-third of the total score. There are eight required moves in a technical program.

triple Salchow—A jump in which the skater takes off from the back inside edge of one foot and lands backward on the outside edge of the opposite foot. The skater performs three turns in the air.

United States Championships—The highest prize in Olympic-eligible competitions in American figure skating.

United States Olympic Committee (USOC)—The governing body for Olympic sports in the United States.

World Championships—An important yearly event in figure skating where top Olympic-level skaters from around the world compete.

World Professional Championships—An important yearly competition for professional skaters who are no longer eligible for the Olympics.

Index

A
artistry, 28
Athletes Village, 38

B
Baiul, Oksana, 31, 39, 43, 61
Bobek, Nicole, 41, 46, 47, 49, 55
Boitano, Brian, 12, 14, 24, 25, 43, 61, 64
Bonaly, Surya, 43, 45, 49
Butyrskaya, Maria, 83, 86, 88

C
Carroll, Frank, 14, 21, 24, 25, 27, 28, 29, 34, 37, 38, 39, 41, 43, 46, 47, 51, 53, 54, 55, 57, 59, 61, 63, 67, 68, 70, 72, 75, 82, 83, 86
Chen, Lu, 42, 49, 54, 59, 60, 61

F
Fratianne, Linda, 21, 24, 28, 61, 74
Free Skate, 12, 43, 46, 47, 49, 54, 59, 60, 69, 83, 88, 89

G
Galindo, Rudy, 56
Goldberg, Shep. 37
Goodwill Games, 43, 79
Grand Prix Finals (Champions Series Final), 8, 57, 85, 89

H
Harding, Tonya, 31, 33, 34, 35, 36, 37, 38, 39, 40, 42
Heart of a Champion, 35
Hughes, Sarah, 80, 82, 85

I
Ice Castle, 20, 21, 36, 53
Ito, Midori, 59

J
James, Derek, 18

K
Kerrigan, Nancy, 31, 32, 33, 34, 35, 36, 37, 38, 39, 40, 42, 74
Kwan, Danny, (father), 16, 23, 37
Kwan, Estella, (mother), 16
Kwan, Karen, (sister), 16, 31, 32, 45, 46, 47, 56, 67
Kwan, Ron, (brother), 16, 31

L
Lake Arrowhead, California, 20, 21, 36, 65
Lillehammer Olympics (1994), 27, 31, 32, 33, 34, 35, 36, 38, 39, 40
Lipinski, Tara, 7, 9, 12, 53, 55, 61, 64, 67, 68, 69, 70, 72, 74, 78

N
Nagano Olympics (1998), 7, 9, 10, 14, 27, 65, 69, 74, 77, 78
Nam, Naomi Nari, 80, 82
Nichol, Lori, 51, 53

P

perfect scores, 12, 14, 28, 60, 61
Petrenko, Victor, 43

S

Salome, 51, 53, 54, 55, 56, 57, 60
Salt Lake City Olympics (2002), 74, 78, 80, 89
Short Program, 10, 11, 42, 43, 46, 47, 57, 59, 60, 68, 69, 75, 83, 88
Skate America, 7, 8, 28, 31, 45, 50, 53, 54, 69, 84, 89
Skate Canada, 7, 54, 85, 89
Slutskaya, Irina, 59, 85, 86, 88, 89
Steinbrenner, George, 20
Sumners, Rosalynn, 31, 69, 74, 86

T

Trenary, Jill, 9, 86

U

UCLA, 83, 84, 86
U.S. Championships (nationals) 7, 9, 10, 19, 24, 31, 33, 34, 38, 45, 46, 55, 56, 69, 80, 82, 85, 86, 89
U.S. Figure Skating Association, 33, 34, 35, 37, 39
U.S. Olympic Committee, 20, 34, 35, 37, 38

W

World Championships, 7, 40, 41, 43, 47, 49, 51, 57, 59, 61, 74, 75, 82, 84, 86, 88, 89

Y

Yamaguchi, Kristi, 31, 86, 89